Our Favorite Casseroles

Copyright 2022, Gooseberry Patch

All rights reserved. No part of this book may be reproduced or utilized in any form or by any means, electronic or mechanical, including photocopying and recording, or by any information storage and retrieval system, without permission in writing from the publisher. Printed in Korea.

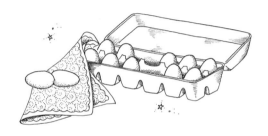

On busy days, a little kitchen prep the night before is really helpful. Whisk up eggs for scrambling, stir together dry ingredients for waffles and lay out tableware ahead of time. In the morning, you'll be a relaxed hostess!

Sausage & Spinach Egg Bake

Makes 6 servings

1 lb. ground Italian pork sausage
1/2 c. onion, chopped
7-oz. jar roasted red peppers,
    drained, chopped and divided
10-oz. pkg. frozen chopped
    spinach, thawed and
    squeezed dry

1 c. all-purpose flour
1/4 c. grated Parmesan cheese
1 t. dried basil
1/2 t. salt
8 eggs, beaten
2 c. milk
1 c. shredded provolone cheese

In a skillet over medium heat, brown sausage with onion; drain. Transfer to a greased 3-quart casserole dish. Sprinkle with half of the red peppers; top with all the spinach. In a large bowl, combine flour, Parmesan cheese and seasonings; set aside. In a separate bowl, whisk together eggs and milk; stir into flour mixture until blended and pour over spinach. Bake, uncovered, at 425 degrees for 15 to 20 minutes, until eggs are set and a knife tip inserted near the center comes out clean. Top with provolone cheese and remaining peppers. Bake for 3 to 5 minutes longer, until cheese is melted. Let stand for 5 minutes before serving.

For the fluffiest scrambled eggs ever, here's a secret...
stir in a pinch of baking powder!

Ham & Cheese Bake

Serves 6 to 8

8-oz. pkg. shredded mozzarella
   cheese
1/2 c. cooked ham, diced
5 eggs, beaten

3/4 c. milk
1/4 t. dried basil
salt and pepper to taste

Layer cheese and ham in a greased 9" pie plate; set aside. In a bowl, whisk together eggs, milk and seasonings; pour into pie plate. Bake at 350 degrees for 30 to 35 minutes. Let stand for 10 minutes before cutting into wedges.

Serving an egg casserole at brunch? Please everyone
by offering two versions...one with bacon or sausage,
and one meatless dish.

Super-Easy Mexican Hashbrown Casserole

Makes 12 to 16 servings

28-oz. pkg. frozen hashbrowns with onions & peppers, thawed
4-oz. can diced green chiles
2 c. shredded Mexican-blend or mild Cheddar cheese, divided

32-oz. container liquid egg substitute
Garnish: salsa
Optional: tortilla chips

Spread potatoes in a lightly greased 13"x9" baking pan. Add chiles and half of cheese. Pour in eggs; sprinkle with remaining cheese. Bake, uncovered, at 350 degrees for 50 minutes, until eggs are set and cheese is melted. Serve with salsa and tortilla chips, if desired.

Whip up a luscious topping to dollop on pancakes and waffles...yum!
Combine 3/4 cup whipping cream, 2 tablespoons softened cream
cheese and one tablespoon powdered sugar. Beat with an
electric mixer on medium speed until soft peaks form. Keep
refrigerated in a small covered crock.

Stuffed French Toast

8 thick slices Italian bread, cubed and divided
2 8-oz. pkgs. reduced-fat cream cheese, cubed
1 to 2 21-oz. cans light cherry, blueberry or peach pie filling

1 doz. eggs, beaten, or equivalent egg substitute
2 c. skim milk
1/3 c. pure maple syrup
1/8 t. nutmeg or cinnamon

Spread half of the bread cubes in a greased 13"x9" baking pan. Scatter cream cheese cubes over bread. If using 2 cans pie filling, partially drain. Spoon pie filling evenly over cream cheese. Top with remaining bread. In a bowl, whisk together remaining ingredients; pour over bread and cheese. Cover and refrigerate overnight. Bake, uncovered, at 375 degrees for 45 minutes, or until hot and eggs are set.

For a great morning time-saver, keep frozen
chopped onions and peppers on hand.

Cheesy Potato Breakfast Casserole *Serves 10 to 12*

6 eggs, beaten
2 c. milk
1 lb. cooked ham, diced
1/4 c. onion, diced
1/4 c. green pepper, diced
3 c. shredded Cheddar cheese
28-oz. pkg frozen diced
   hashbrowns, thawed

In a large bowl, whisk together eggs and milk. Stir in ham, onion, green pepper, and cheese; fold in thawed hashbrowns. Pour mixture into a lightly greased 13"x9" baking pan. Cover with aluminum foil. Bake at 350 degrees for 45 minutes. Uncover; bake for another 30 minutes, or until eggs are set.

An apron collection is a whimsical (and practical!) addition to your kitchen. Look for vintage styles at thrift shops and tag sales...hang them from pegs in the kitchen. Everyone can tie on their own ruffled, polka-dotted or flowered favorite whenever they help out in the kitchen.

Brunch Crescent Casserole

Makes 10 servings

2 8-oz. tubes refrigerated
   crescent rolls
1 c. baked turkey ham, cubed
6 green onions, sliced thin
5 eggs, lightly beaten
1 c. milk

1 c. fat-free half-and-half
1 t. salt
1 t. pepper
8-oz. pkg. shredded mozzarella
   cheese

Separate rolls; roll up each roll crescent-style. Arrange rolls in 2 long rows in a greased 13"x9" baking pan. Top with ham and onions; set aside. In a bowl, whisk together remaining ingredients except cheese; fold in cheese and spoon over rolls. Bake, uncovered, at 375 degrees for 20 to 25 minutes, until golden and cheese is melted. Cut into squares.

Try something new...warm apple pie filling is delicious
spooned over individual bowls of oatmeal.

Amish Baked Oatmeal

Serves 6 to 8

1/4 c. butter, softened
1 egg, beaten
1/2 c. sugar
1 t. baking powder
1/2 t. salt

1/2 c. milk
1 t. vanilla extract
2 T. oil
1-3/4 c. quick-cooking oats,
    uncooked

Mix together all ingredients except oats until smooth; pour into a greased
13"x9" baking pan. Stir in oats. Bake, uncovered, at 350 degrees for
30 to 35 minutes.

Start a collection of retro jelly-jar juice glasses...
their fun designs and bright colors will make everyone
smile at breakfast time.

Sausage & Pecan Casserole

Serves 10

8-oz. pkg. pork breakfast
    sausage links
16-oz. loaf cinnamon bread, cubed
6 eggs, beaten
1-1/2 c. half-and-half

1-1/2 c. milk
1 t. vanilla extract
1/2 t. cinnamon
1/2 t. nutmeg
1 c. chopped pecans

Brown sausages in a skillet over medium heat; drain and thinly slice. Place bread cubes in a 13"x9" baking pan sprayed with non-stick vegetable spray. Top with sausages and set aside. In a large bowl, beat together remaining ingredients except pecans; fold in pecans. Pour egg mixture over sausage; press down gently. Cover and refrigerate overnight. In the morning, make Topping; sprinkle over top. Bake, uncovered, at 350 degrees for 35 minutes, or until bubbly and eggs are set.

Topping:

1 c. brown sugar, packed
1 c. chopped pecans

1/2 c. butter, softened
2 T. maple syrup

Stir together all ingredients with a fork until crumbly.

Planning a midday brunch? Along with breakfast foods like baked eggs, coffee cake and cereal, offer a light, savory main dish for those who have already enjoyed breakfast.

Farmhouse Chicken Pie

Makes 5 to 6 servings

9-inch pie crust, unbaked
1/2 bunch broccoli, chopped
3/4 c. shredded Swiss cheese
5 slices bacon, crisply cooked
   and crumbled
1-1/2 to 2 c. cooked chicken,
   shredded

2 eggs, beaten
2-1/4 c. milk
1-1/2 T. all-purpose flour
1/8 t. nutmeg
1/8 t salt

Bake pie crust according to package directions. Meanwhile, place broccoli in a saucepan with a small amount of water. Cook over low heat until tender; drain well. To assemble, layer cheese, bacon, broccoli and chicken in baked pie crust; set aside. In a bowl, combine remaining ingredients; whisk together well and pour over top. Bake at 350 degrees for one hour, or until bubbly and crust is golden. Let stand several minutes; cut into wedges.

Planning an appetizers-only event? You'll want to serve
at least 5 different dishes...allow 2 to 3 servings
of each per person.

Buffalo Wing Dip

Serves 10

2 8-oz. pkgs. cream cheese, softened
15-oz. jar chunky blue cheese salad dressing
12-oz. bottle chicken wing sauce
2 boneless, skinless chicken breasts, cooked and shredded
8-oz. pkg. shredded Cheddar Jack cheese
tortilla chips or assorted crackers

In a bowl, blend together cream cheese and salad dressing until smooth. Spread in the bottom of an ungreased 8"x8" baking pan. Combine sauce and chicken; spoon over cream cheese mixture. Sprinkle with shredded cheese. Bake, uncovered, at 350 degrees for 20 minutes, or until cheese is melted and dip is heated through. Serve with tortilla chips or crackers.

A 250-degree oven keeps hot appetizers toasty
until you're ready to serve them.

Jalapeño Cheese Squares

Serves 4 to 6

2 c. shredded Cheddar cheese
2 c. shredded Monterey Jack
    cheese
3/4 c. pickled jalapeño pepper
    slices, drained

2 eggs, beaten
1/2 c. all-purpose flour
12-oz. can evaporated milk

Mix together cheeses in a large bowl; spread half of mixture in a greased 13"x9" baking pan. Top with peppers; sprinkle remaining cheese mixture over top. In a bowl, stir together eggs, flour and evaporated milk. Pour batter over cheese mixture. Bake, uncovered, at 350 degrees for 25 to 30 minutes, until set and cheese is melted. Let cool slightly; cut into squares.

Mix up some salsa in a *jiffy!* Pour a 15-ounce can of
stewed tomatoes, several slices of canned jalapeños
and a teaspoon or 2 of the jalapeño juice into a blender.
Cover and process to the desired consistency.

Hot & Melty Taco Dip

Makes 8 servings

16-oz. can refried beans
1-1/2 oz. pkg. taco seasoning mix
16-oz. container sour cream
8-oz. pkg. cream cheese, softened
16-oz. jar salsa
8-oz. pkg. shredded sharp
    Cheddar cheese

Garnish: shredded lettuce,
    chopped tomatoes, sliced black
    olives, jalapeño peppers,
    green onions
scoop-type tortilla chips

In a bowl, combine refried beans with taco seasoning. Spread in the bottom of a lightly greased 13"x9" glass baking pan; set aside. In a separate bowl, blend sour cream and cream cheese; spread over bean layer. Spoon salsa over sour cream layer; sprinkle cheese on top. Bake, uncovered, at 350 degrees for about 25 minutes, until beans are warmed through and cheese is melted. Garnish with desired toppings. Serve warm with tortilla chips.

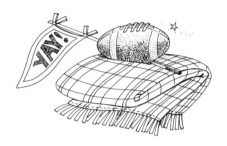

Keep a keen eye out for woolly stadium blankets at local flea markets and tag sales. Not only are they great for keeping you and friends toasty during the game, they'll fit right in as clever tablecloths at your next tailgate party.

Championship Artichoke Dip

Makes 7 cups

2 c. grated Parmesan cheese
2 c. shredded Mozzarella cheese
1 c. mayonnaise
2 cloves garlic, minced

16-oz. can artichoke hearts,
   drained and finely chopped
1/4 c. green onions, chopped
assorted crackers

Combine all ingredients except green onions and crackers in a lightly greased 8"x8" baking pan; mix thoroughly. Bake, uncovered, at 375 degrees for 45 minutes, or until hot and bubbly. Sprinkle with onions; serve warm with crackers.

When you need to chill lots of juice boxes, cans of soda pop or bottles of water, you'll find they chill more quickly on ice than in the refrigerator. Just add beverages to an ice-filled cooler or galvanized tub. You'll save valuable refrigerator space too!

Papa Dale's Hot Chicken Dip

Makes 10 to 12 servings

8-oz. pkg. cream cheese, softened
1/2 c. blue cheese salad dressing
1/2 c. crumbled blue cheese
1/2 c. hot pepper sauce

2 12-oz. cans white meat chicken,
  well drained
assorted crackers

In an ungreased one-quart casserole dish, blend cream cheese, salad dressing, blue cheese and hot sauce. Stir in chicken. Bake, uncovered, at 350 degrees for 25 minutes, or until hot and bubbly. Serve warm with crackers.

Whip up a fresh salad for dinner tonight. Toss together mixed greens, cherry tomatoes and thinly sliced red onion in a salad bowl. Whisk together 1/4 cup each of balsamic vinegar and olive oil, then drizzle over salad...so zesty!

Pizza Potato Puff Casserole

1 lb. ground beef
1/4 c. onion, chopped
10-3/4 oz. can cream of
mushroom soup
8-oz. can pizza sauce

12 to 15 slices pepperoni
1/2 c. green pepper, chopped
1 c. shredded mozzarella cheese
16-oz. pkg. frozen potato puffs

Brown beef and onion in a skillet over medium-high heat; drain. Stir in soup. Spoon beef mixture into a lightly greased 8"x8" baking pan. Spoon pizza sauce evenly over beef mixture; arrange pepperoni and green pepper over sauce. Sprinkle with cheese; arrange potato puffs over top. Cover with aluminum foil; bake at 375 degrees for 30 minutes. Uncover; bake an additional 15 to 20 minutes, until heated through.

While the main dish simmers, turn leftover mashed potatoes into twice-baked potatoes. Stir in minced onion, crumbled bacon, sour cream and shredded cheese to taste. Pat into mini casserole dishes. Bake at 350 degrees until hot and golden...scrumptious!

One-Dish Steak Supper

Makes 6 servings

1-1/2 lbs. beef top round steak,
    cut into serving-size pieces
salt and pepper to taste
4 T. butter, sliced
4 T. Worcestershire sauce
4 potatoes, peeled and thickly
    sliced

1 onion, sliced and separated
    into rings
5 carrots, peeled and sliced
1 green pepper, cut into rings

Season steak on all sides with salt and pepper. Arrange in a lightly greased 13"x9" baking pan. Dot with butter; drizzle Worcestershire sauce over steak. Arrange vegetables on top. Cover with heavy aluminum foil. Bake at 350 degrees for 1-1/4 hours. Remove foil; bake another 15 minutes, or until steak is browned.

For simple table decorations, place round pebbles in the bottom of Mason jars and fill with water. Then tuck in bunches of sweet daisies or sunflowers and tie a bow around jar necks with jute.

Chuckwagon Casserole

1 lb. lean ground beef
1/2 c. onion, chopped
1/2 c. green pepper, chopped
15-1/2 oz. can mild chili beans
  in sauce

3/4 c. barbecue sauce
1/2 t. salt
8-1/2 oz. pkg. cornbread mix
11-oz. can sweet corn & diced
  peppers, drained

In a skillet over medium heat, cook beef, onion and pepper until no longer pink; drain. Stir in chili beans, barbecue sauce and salt; bring to a boil. Spoon into a lightly greased 13"x9" baking pan and set aside. Prepare cornbread mix according to package directions; stir corn into batter and spoon over beef mixture. Bake, uncovered, at 400 degrees for 30 minutes, or until golden.

Mix up your own Italian seasoning for pasta dishes, soups, salad and garlic bread. A good basic blend is 2 tablespoons each of dried oregano, thyme, basil, marjoram and rosemary... add or subtract to suit your family's taste. Store in a big shaker jar.

Herby Bubble Bread

Serves 6 to 8

3 1-lb. loaves frozen bread dough, thawed but still chilled
1/4 c. olive oil
3 T. Italian salad dressing mix

1 c. shredded sharp Cheddar cheese
1 t. garlic, minced
1 red onion, finely chopped

Cut dough into one-inch cubes; place in a large bowl. Pour remaining ingredients over dough. Using your hands, toss until dough cubes are coated. Transfer dough cubes to a greased 13"x9" baking pan. Place in a warm area; cover and let rise until double in size. Bake at 350 degrees for 20 to 25 minutes, until golden.

Whenever just a little onion is needed for a casserole recipe, use green onions instead. Easily cut with kitchen scissors, they add a light onion flavor with no leftover onion to store.

Hearty Stuffed Pepper Casserole

Serves 4 to 6

2-1/2 c. herb-flavored stuffing
    mix, divided
1 T. butter, melted
1 lb. ground beef
1/2 c. onion, chopped

14-1/2 oz. can whole tomatoes,
    chopped
8-oz. can corn, drained
salt and pepper to taste
2 green peppers, quartered

Mix together 1/4 cup dry stuffing mix and butter; set aside. Brown beef
and onion in a skillet over medium-high heat; drain. Stir in tomatoes with
juice, corn, salt and pepper; add remaining stuffing mix. Arrange green
peppers in an ungreased 2-quart casserole dish; spoon beef mixture over
top. Cover and bake at 400 degrees for 25 minutes. Sprinkle with reserved
stuffing mixture. Bake, uncovered, for 5 additional minutes, or until
peppers are tender.

Toss cooked pasta with a little olive oil and set aside to keep warm. When it's time to add the pasta to a favorite casserole recipe, you'll find the oil has kept the pasta from sticking together.

Company Noodle Casserole

Makes 6 servings

4 c. wide egg noodles, uncooked
1 lb. ground beef
1/3 c. onion, chopped
2 8-oz. cans tomato sauce

1 c. cottage cheese
8-oz. pkg. cream cheese, softened
1/4 c. sour cream

Cook noodles according to package directions; drain. Meanwhile, in a skillet over medium heat, brown beef with onion; drain. Stir in tomato sauce; simmer until heated through. Combine remaining ingredients in a bowl; blend well and aside. In a greased 3-quart casserole dish, layer half each of noodles, beef mixture and cottage cheese mixture. Repeat layering. Bake, uncovered, at 350 degrees for 40 minutes, or until bubbly and golden.

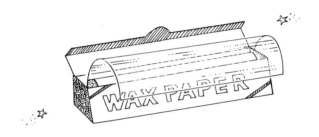

Mix flour and seasonings for dredging meat on a piece
of wax paper...when you're done, just toss it away.

42

Baked Steak with Gravy

Makes 6 to 8 servings

1 c. all-purpose flour
1/8 t. salt
1/8 t. pepper
6 to 8 beef cube steaks
1 t. butter

2 10-3/4 oz. cans golden
  mushroom soup
2-1/2 c. water
4-oz. can sliced mushrooms,
  drained

Mix flour, salt and pepper in a shallow bowl; dredge steaks in mixture. Melt butter in a skillet over medium heat; add steaks and brown on both sides. Arrange steaks in a lightly greased 13"x9" baking pan; set aside. Stir together soup, water and mushrooms; spoon over steaks. Cover with aluminum foil. Bake at 325 degrees for 45 to 50 minutes. Uncover; bake 15 minutes more.

Flea markets offer an amazing variety of table serving
pieces for entertaining! Watch for vintage china, casseroles
and jelly-jar glasses to add old-fashioned charm
to your dinner table.

Chicken Comfort Casserole

7-oz. pkg. chicken-flavored rice vermicelli mix
4 boneless, skinless chicken breasts, cooked and cubed
1/4 c. butter
1/2 c. onion, chopped
1/2 c. green pepper, chopped
1/2 c. celery, chopped
2 10-3/4 oz. cans cream of chicken soup
1 c. shredded Cheddar cheese

Prepare rice vermicelli mix according to package directions. Toss with chicken; set aside. Melt butter in a skillet over medium heat; sauté onion, pepper and celery until tender. Combine with rice mixture and soup; spoon into a greased 13"x9" baking pan. Top with cheese; bake at 400 degrees for 20 minutes.

Purchase a bundle of wheat straw at a craft store.
Arrange a few stalks on each folded napkin for a
beautiful yet simple reminder of a bountiful harvest.

Turkey-Almond Casserole

Serves 6

2 10-3/4 oz. cans cream of
   mushroom soup
1/2 c. mayonnaise
1/2 c. sour cream
2 T. onion, chopped
2 T. lemon juice
1 t. salt
1/2 t. pepper
5 c. cooked turkey, cubed

3 c. cooked rice
4 stalks celery, chopped
8-oz. can sliced water chestnuts,
   drained
1-1/4 c. sliced almonds, divided
1-1/2 c. round buttery cracker
   crumbs
1/3 c. butter, melted

Combine soup, mayonnaise, sour cream, onion, lemon juice, salt and
pepper in a large bowl; mix well. Stir in turkey, rice, celery, water chestnuts
and one cup almonds. Transfer to a greased 13"x9" baking pan; set aside.
Mix remaining almonds, cracker crumbs and butter; sprinkle over top.
Bake, uncovered, at 350 degrees for 35 to 40 minutes, until bubbly
and golden.

A loaf of a favorite bread is such a thoughtful gift...
why not include the recipe along with a pretty vintage
tea towel tied with a bow?

Dilly Casserole Bread

Makes one loaf

1 env. active dry yeast
1/4 c. warm water
1 c. cottage cheese
2 T. sugar
1 T. dried, minced onion
1/4 t. baking soda

1 egg, beaten
2 T. butter, softened and divided
2 t. dill weed, divided
1-1/2 t. salt, divided
2-1/4 to 2-1/2 c. all-purpose flour

Soften yeast in very warm water, about 110 to 115 degrees; set aside for 5 minutes. In a large bowl, combine cottage cheese, sugar, onion, baking soda, egg, one tablespoon butter, one teaspoon dill weed, one teaspoon salt and yeast mixture. Stir in enough flour to make a stiff dough. Cover and let rise until double in bulk, about 40 minutes. Stir dough down; place in a greased 9"x5" loaf pan. Let rise again for 40 minutes. Bake at 350 degrees for 35 to 40 minutes, until golden. Brush with remaining butter; sprinkle with remaining dill weed and salt.

Casseroles spell comfort food, but what if the recipe is large and your family is small? Simple... just divide the ingredients into 2 small dishes and freeze one for later!

Crunchy Biscuit Chicken

Serves 4 to 6

2 c. cooked chicken, diced
10-3/4 oz. can cream of
    chicken soup
14-1/2 oz. can green beans
1 c. shredded Cheddar cheese
4-oz. can sliced mushrooms
1/2 c. mayonnaise-type salad
    dressing

1 t. lemon juice
10-oz. tube refrigerated flaky
    biscuits
1 to 2 T. butter, melted
1/4 c. Cheddar cheese croutons,
    crushed

In a medium saucepan over medium heat, combine chicken, soup, beans, cheese, mushrooms, salad dressing and lemon juice. Stir well; cook until hot and bubbly. Spoon hot chicken mixture into an ungreased 13"x9" baking pan. Separate biscuit dough into 10 biscuits; arrange biscuits over chicken mixture. Brush each biscuit with butter; sprinkle with croutons. Bake, uncovered, at 375 degrees for 25 to 30 minutes, until deeply golden.

Get out the tiki torches and grass skirts when serving Polynesian Chicken! Play Hawaiian music, make paper flower leis and make it a family dinner to remember.

Polynesian Chicken

Makes 4 servings

4 chicken breasts
1 c. teriyaki marinade
8-oz. can crushed pineapple

8-oz. can whole-berry
cranberry sauce

Combine chicken and marinade in a large plastic zipping bag; seal bag. Refrigerate for several hours, turning bag once or twice. Drain, discarding marinade. Arrange chicken in a greased 13"x9" baking pan. Spoon pineapple with juice and cranberry sauce over chicken. Bake, uncovered, at 350 degrees for one hour, or until chicken is golden and juices run clear.

It's easy to separate frozen vegetables. Put them in a colander and pour on hot water. Let water drain into the sink and add veggies to casserole ingredients.

Turkey-Broccoli Casserole
Makes 8 to 10 servings

16-oz. pkg. frozen chopped
   broccoli
2 lbs. ground turkey
8-oz. pkg. sliced mushrooms
1 onion, chopped
salt and pepper to taste

2 10-3/4 oz. cans cream of celery
   soup
16-oz. container sour cream
16-oz. pkg. shredded Monterey
   Jack cheese

Cook broccoli according to package directions; drain well. Meanwhile, in a
large deep skillet over medium heat, brown turkey with mushrooms and
onion; drain. Season turkey mixture with salt and pepper; stir in soup and
sour cream. Reduce heat to low; heat through. Transfer turkey mixture to
a lightly greased 13"x9" baking pan. Layer evenly with broccoli; top with
cheese. Bake, uncovered, at 350 degrees for one hour, or until bubbly and
lightly golden.

Casseroles are ideal for toting to neighborhood
block parties. You'll enjoy catching up with friends while
the kids race around playing games. You might even
want to set them up a table for face painting...how fun!

One-Dish Chicken & Gravy

Serves 4 to 5

1/4 c. butter, melted
3 lbs. chicken
1/4 c. all-purpose flour
8 pearl onions
4-oz. jar mushroom stems
  and pieces, drained
2/3 c. evaporated milk

10-3/4 oz. can cream of
  mushroom soup
1 c. pasteurized processed cheese
  spread, cubed
3/4 t. salt
1/8 t. pepper
Garnish: paprika

Spread butter in a 12"x8" baking pan; set aside. Coat chicken pieces
with flour; arrange in baking pan skin-side down in a single layer. Bake,
uncovered, at 425 degrees for 30 minutes. Turn chicken over; bake an
additional 15 to 20 minutes, until golden. Top with onions and mushrooms;
set aside. Combine evaporated milk, soup, cheese, salt and pepper; spoon
over chicken. Sprinkle with paprika; cover with aluminum foil. Reduce
oven to 325 degrees and bake an additional 15 to 20 minutes.

Whip up a gourmet salad in seconds! Purchase a bag of mixed salad greens and toss in fruit, nuts and grated cheese. Top off the salad with a drizzle of raspberry vinaigrette and toss.

Chicken Noodle Bake

Serves 6 to 8

12-oz. pkg. wide egg noodles, cooked
3/4 lb. pasteurized processed cheese spread, melted
2 boneless, skinless chicken breasts, cooked and cubed

2 10-3/4 oz. cans cream of chicken soup
1 c. chicken broth
1 c. dry bread crumbs
1/4 c. plus 2 T. butter, melted

In a large bowl, combine all ingredients except crumbs and butter; mix well. Transfer to a greased 13"x9" baking pan and set aside. Combine bread crumbs and butter; mix well to coat and sprinkle over chicken mixture. Bake, uncovered, at 350 degrees for 30 to 40 minutes, until bubbly and golden.

A savory roast chicken from the deli is the busy cook's
secret ingredient! The chicken is already cooked and
ready for whatever recipe you decide to make...
just slice, chop or shred as needed.

Party Paella Casserole

Serves 8

2 8-oz. pkgs. yellow rice, uncooked
1 lb. medium shrimp, cleaned
1 T. fresh lemon juice
1/2 t. salt
1/4 t. pepper
2 cloves garlic, minced
1-1/2 T. olive oil
2-1/2 lb. lemon & garlic deli rotisserie chicken, coarsely shredded

5 green onions, chopped
8-oz. container sour cream
1 c. frozen peas, thawed
1 c. green olives with pimentos, coarsely chopped
1-1/2 c. shredded Monterey Jack cheese
1/2 t. smoked Spanish paprika

Prepare rice according to package directions. Remove from heat and let cool 30 minutes; fluff with a fork. Meanwhile, in a bowl, toss shrimp with lemon juice, salt and pepper. In a large non-stick skillet, sauté seasoned shrimp and garlic in hot oil for 2 minutes, or just until done. Remove from heat. Combine shredded chicken, cooked rice, green onions, sour cream and peas in a large bowl; toss well. Add shrimp and olives, tossing gently. Spoon mixture into a greased 13"x9" baking pan. Combine cheese and paprika, tossing well; sprinkle over casserole. Bake, uncovered, at 400 degrees for 15 minutes or just until cheese is melted and casserole is heated through.

Change the flavor of a seafood casserole just by trying a different type of fish in the recipe. Mild-flavored fish would be cod, flounder or haddock, while stronger flavors would include swordfish, tuna, salmon or mackerel.

New-Fangled Tuna Penne Casserole

Serves 2

2-1/4 c. whole-wheat penne
   pasta, uncooked
1/2 lb. sliced mushrooms
2 green onions, minced
1/4 c. fresh Italian parsley, minced
1 to 2 6-oz. cans tuna, drained

8-oz. container sour cream
1/2 c. light mayonnaise
2 t. Dijon mustard
Optional: 2 T. dry white wine
1/2 c. shredded Cheddar cheese

Cook pasta according to package directions; drain and return to pan.
Meanwhile, spray a skillet with non-stick vegetable spray. Add mushrooms,
onions and parsley. Cook over medium heat until mushrooms are tender,
about 5 minutes. Add tuna; cook until heated through. Stir tuna mixture
into pasta; blend in sour cream, mayonnaise, mustard and wine, if using.
Spread in a lightly greased 2-quart casserole dish. Top with cheese. Bake,
uncovered, at 375 degrees for 30 minutes.

Try serving homemade fruit dip with apple slices, grapes, melon wedges and strawberries. What a refreshing side dish and this dip recipe is a snap! Stir together a 16-ounce container of sour cream, 1/4 cup sugar and 2 teaspoons vanilla extract.

Crab & Shrimp Casserole

Serves 4 to 6

2 8-oz. cans crabmeat, drained
2 4-oz. cans tiny shrimp, drained
2 c. celery, chopped
1 green pepper, chopped
1 onion, chopped
1 T. Worcestershire sauce

1 t. sugar
1 c. mayonnaise
salt and pepper to taste
1 c. soft bread crumbs, buttered
2 T. lemon juice
Garnish: thin lemon slices

Mix together all ingredients except bread crumbs, lemon juice and garnish.
Transfer to a greased 13"x9" baking pan. Spread bread crumbs over
casserole. Bake, uncovered, at 350 degrees for 30 to 45 minutes, until
heated through. Sprinkle lemon juice over casserole; garnish with
lemon slices.

SEAFOOD
fresh
catch
DAILY!

To keep fish its freshest, put it into a tightly sealed
plastic zipping bag, then place inside a bowl filled with ice.
Refrigerate and use within a day or two.

Dijon Salmon Bake

Serves 4

6-oz. pkg. baby spinach, cooked,
    well-drained and shredded
1-3/4 c. cooked rice
1/2 t. salt, divided
3/4 c. sour cream
1 egg, beaten
1 T. Dijon mustard

3 T. grated Parmesan & Romano
    cheese, divided
1 lb. boneless, skinless salmon
    filet, sliced 1/2-inch thick
    on the diagonal
1/2 t. water

Combine spinach, rice and 1/4 teaspoon salt in a large bowl; set aside.
Whisk together sour cream, egg, mustard, 2 tablespoons cheese,
remaining salt and pepper in a small bowl. Add all except 4 tablespoons
sour cream mixture to spinach mixture and stir to coat. Spoon into a
greased 1-1/2 quart casserole dish; top with salmon. Add water to
remaining sour cream mixture; mix well and drizzle over salmon. Top
with remaining cheese. Bake, uncovered, at 350 degrees for 30 minutes.
Let stand 5 minutes before serving.

To freshen cooking pans after preparing fish in them, simply fill the pan with equal parts vinegar and water. Bring to a boil for 5 minutes, let cool, then wash the pan with hot, soapy water.

Montana Baked Halibut

Serves 6 to 8

3 lbs. halibut fillets
3 T. butter, softened and divided
salt and pepper to taste
4 slices bacon

1/2 c. grated Parmesan cheese
1 c. sour cream
2 t. lemon juice
1/3 c. cornbread croutons, crushed

Brush halibut with 2 tablespoons softened butter; season with salt and pepper. Arrange bacon slices in an ungreased 13"x9" baking pan; arrange halibut over bacon. Mix together cheese, sour cream and lemon juice; spread over halibut and set aside. Melt remaining butter in a saucepan over low heat; remove from heat. Add croutons and toss to coat; sprinkle over halibut. Bake, uncovered, at 350 degrees for 25 to 30 minutes, depending on thickness of halibut.

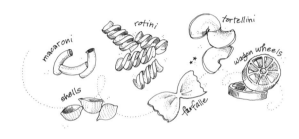

macaroni

rotini

tortellini

shells

wagon wheels

farfalle

Pasta shapes like bowties, seashells, wagon wheels and corkscrew-shaped cavatappi all work well in casseroles... why not give a favorite casserole a whole new look?

Penne with Sausage & Cheese

Makes 6 servings

12-oz. pkg. penne pasta,
  uncooked
1 lb. hot or mild Italian ground
  pork sausage
3 cloves garlic, chopped
26-oz. jar tomato & basil spaghetti
  sauce

1/2 t. red pepper flakes
1/2 t. salt
1/2 t. pepper
1 c. shredded mozzarella cheese
Garnish: grated Parmesan cheese,
  chopped fresh parsley

Cook pasta according to package directions; drain. Meanwhile, in a skillet over medium heat, cook sausage until browned; drain. Add garlic and cook until tender, about 2 minutes. Stir in sauce and seasonings. Stir sauce mixture into cooked pasta; transfer mixture to a greased 12"x8" baking pan. Top with mozzarella cheese. Bake, covered, at 375 degrees for 25 to 30 minutes, until bubbly and cheese is melted. Sprinkle with Parmesan cheese and parsley.

Even the simplest meal is special when shared. Why not invite
a dinner guest or two the next time you have a tasty dinner
in the oven? The menu doesn't need to be fancy...it's sure
to be appreciated!

Ham & Cauliflower Au Gratin

Makes 6 to 8 servings

2 10-oz. pkgs. frozen cauliflower,
  thawed and drained
1-1/4 c. smoked ham, diced
10-3/4 oz. can Cheddar cheese
  soup
1/4 c. milk
2/3 c. biscuit baking mix
2 to 3 T. butter, softened
1/2 t. nutmeg
dried parsley and paprika to taste

Arrange cauliflower in a lightly greased 13"x9" baking pan; sprinkle with ham. Whisk together soup and milk until smooth; spoon over ham. Toss together biscuit mix, butter and nutmeg with a fork until crumbly; sprinkle over soup mixture. Sprinkle with parsley and paprika. Bake, uncovered, at 400 degrees until cauliflower is tender and topping is golden, 20 to 25 minutes.

Sprinkle a flavorful seasoning onto casserole dishes before baking. Combine 1/4 cup coarse salt with 2 to 4 tablespoons mixed ground spices. Try combinations such as caraway seed and pepper, thyme and sesame seed or chili powder and dried oregano.

Zucchini & Sausage Casserole

Serves 8 to 10

1 lb. sweet Italian ground pork
    sausage, browned and drained
8-1/2 oz. pkg. cornbread mix
10-oz. pkg. frozen corn, thawed
3 c. zucchini, shredded
1 onion, finely chopped

2 eggs, beaten
1-1/2 t. garlic, minced
1/2 t. dried dill weed
1/2 t. salt
1-1/4 c. shredded Cheddar cheese,
    divided

Combine browned sausage and dry cornbread mix in a lightly greased 2-quart casserole dish. Add remaining ingredients, setting aside 1/4 cup cheese for topping. Mix gently. Bake, uncovered, at 350 degrees for about 50 minutes, until a knife tip inserted in the center comes out clean. Top with reserved cheese; return to oven long enough to melt the cheese.

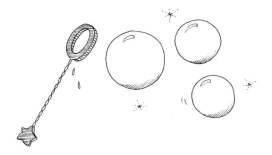

While dinner is in the oven, enjoy some time lazily blowing bubbles with the kids. The best bubble solution is a homemade recipe of 10 cups water plus 4 cups dish-washing liquid and one cup corn syrup.

Beans & Wieners Waikiki

Serves 6

20-oz. can pineapple slices,
    drained and juice reserved
2 T. butter
1/3 c. green pepper, coarsely
    chopped
1/4 c. onion, chopped

8 hot dogs, cut into chunks
2 T. vinegar
1 T. soy sauce
1/3 c. catsup
1/3 c. brown sugar, packed
15-oz. can pork & beans

Cut pineapple into chunks, reserving 3 or 4 rings for garnish; set aide. Melt butter in a skillet over medium heat. Sauté green pepper, onion, pineapple chunks and hot dog chunks until golden; simmer for 5 minutes. Add reserved pineapple juice, vinegar, soy sauce, catsup and brown sugar; cook and stir until bubbly. Pour pork & beans into a lightly greased 13"x9" baking pan. Add pineapple mixture; stir gently to blend. Halve reserved pineapple slices; arrange on top. Bake, uncovered, at 350 degrees for 30 minutes, or until hot and bubbly.

Laughter is brightest where food is best.

—Irish Proverb

Savory Pork Tenderloin

Serves 4 to 6

3 potatoes, peeled and
   thinly sliced
1-1/4 c. milk, divided
salt and pepper to taste
1-1/2 c. soft bread crumbs
1/2 t. salt

1/4 t. dried sage
2 T. plus 2 t. butter, diced
   and divided
2 T. onion, minced
1 lb. pork tenderloin, sliced
   1/2-inch thick

Layer potato slices in a well-greased 2-quart casserole dish. Add one cup milk; season with salt and pepper. Combine remaining milk, bread crumbs, salt, sage, 2 teaspoons butter and onion; spread over potatoes and set aside. Flatten pork slices with a mallet until 1/4-inch thick. Arrange over bread crumbs and dot with remaining butter. Bake, covered, at 350 degrees for 1-1/2 hours.

Giant ice cubes! Add layers of thinly sliced lemons, limes and oranges in muffin cups. Fill each cup halfway with water and freeze. So pretty floating in a pitcher of tea, lemonade or ice water.

Pork Chop Bake

Makes 4 to 6 serving-size

1 T. oil
4 to 6 pork chops
10-3/4 oz. can cream of
    mushroom soup with
    roasted garlic
1 c. sour cream

1/4 c. milk
3 stalks celery, chopped
1/4 c. red pepper, diced
4 c. potatoes, peeled and diced
salt and pepper to taste
Optional: dried parsley, paprika

Heat oil in a large skillet over medium heat; add pork chops and cook until golden on both sides. Remove from skillet and set aside. Mix together soup, sour cream, milk, celery and red pepper; set aside. Arrange potatoes evenly in a lightly greased 13"x9" baking pan; spoon soup mixture over potatoes. Arrange pork chops on top of soup; press down into soup, leaving tops exposed. Season with salt, pepper, parsley and paprika, as desired. Cover and bake at 375 degrees for 1-1/4 hours.

It's a lovely thing...everyone sitting down together, sharing food.

—Alice May Brock

Casserole Onion Bread

Serves 8 to 10

1 c. milk
3 T. sugar
1-1/2 T. butter
3/4 c. warm water

1 env. active dry yeast
1-1/2 oz. pkg. onion soup mix
4 c. all-purpose flour

Heat milk in a saucepan over medium heat just until boiling. Pour into a bowl; add sugar and butter. Cool slightly. Heat water until very warm, about 110 to 115 degrees; add yeast and stir until dissolved. Add yeast mixture to milk mixture; add soup mix and flour. Stir for 2 minutes, or until well mixed. Cover bowl with a tea towel; let rise for 45 minutes, until double in bulk. Stir dough down; beat vigorously for 30 seconds. Turn into a greased 1-1/2 quart casserole dish. Bake, uncovered, at 375 degrees for 45 to 55 minutes. Tent with aluminum foil if top is browning too fast. Cool in pan on wire rack for 5 minutes; turn upside-down to remove.

Whip up mix & match napkin rings from ribbon scraps...
so simple. For each ring, fold a 6-inch length of ribbon
in half, right sides facing, and sew ends together with
a 1/4-inch seam allowance. Turn the rings right side out,
and slip them around rolled napkins.

Herbed Sausage Quiche

Serves 8

9-inch frozen pie crust, thawed
1 c. ground pork breakfast
   sausage, browned and drained
3 eggs, beaten
1 c. whipping cream
1 c. shredded Cheddar cheese

1-1/2 t. Italian seasoning
1/4 t. salt
1/4 t. pepper
2 sprigs fresh rosemary, chopped
   and divided

Bake pie crust according to package directions. In a bowl, mix together remaining ingredients, reserving half of rosemary for garnish; spread into crust. Bake at 450 degrees for 15 minutes; reduce heat to 350 degrees. Cover with aluminum foil and bake for 10 more minutes or until set. Garnish with remaining rosemary. Cut into wedges to serve.

Cut the corner from a paper envelope, then snip off
the tip to create a tiny funnel perfect for filling
salt & pepper shakers.

Roasted Veggies & Penne Pasta   *Makes 6 to 8 servings*

16-oz. pkg. penne pasta,
   uncooked
2 zucchini, quartered lengthwise
   and sliced 1-inch thick
2 yellow squash, quartered
   lengthwise and sliced
   1-inch thick
2 red peppers, cut into 1-inch
   squares

1 onion, cut into 1-inch squares
1 to 2 T. olive oil
kosher salt to taste
3 c. shredded mozzarella cheese,
   divided
1/4 c. plus 2 T. grated Parmesan
   cheese, divided

Cook pasta according to package directions, just until tender; drain.
Meanwhile, combine vegetables in a greased 13"x9" baking pan. Drizzle
with oil and season with salt. Bake, uncovered, at 425 degrees for 15 to
20 minutes, stirring once or twice, until golden and caramelized. Add
cooked pasta to vegetable mixture along with 2 cups mozzarella cheese
and 1/4 cup Parmesan cheese. Toss to mix well; sprinkle with remaining
cheeses. Return to oven for 5 minutes, or until cheese melts.

Noodles are not only amusing, but delicious.

—Julia Child

Susan's Vegetable Lasagna

2 to 3 t. olive oil
6 c. vegetables, diced, such as
 zucchini, yellow squash,
 carrots, broccoli, red peppers,
 mushrooms
1 onion, diced
2 cloves garlic, minced
2 to 6 T. soy sauce or
 Worcestershire sauce
pepper to taste

1/2 t. dried basil
1/2 t. dried oregano
26-oz. jar marinara sauce, divided
9-oz. pkg. no-boil lasagna
 noodles, uncooked and divided
1 c. ricotta cheese
1 c. grated Parmesan cheese
1-1/2 c. shredded mozzarella
 cheese

Over medium-high heat, drizzle oil into a skillet. Add vegetables and onion; stir-fry until onion turns translucent. Add garlic and soy or Worcestershire sauce; continue cooking until vegetables are tender. Season with pepper, basil and oregano. Spread 1/2 cup marinara sauce in an ungreased 13"x9" baking pan. Arrange 1/3 of the noodles over sauce; top with half of ricotta cheese and half of Parmesan cheese. Top with half of the vegetables. Repeat layering, ending with remaining noodles, remaining sauce and all of the mozzarella cheese. Bake, uncovered, at 350 degrees for 25 to 30 minutes, until hot and bubbly.

Corral kitchen utensils with a playful candy wrapper pail. Apply découpage medium to the pail with a foam brush, smooth on wrappers, and then coat the wrappers with another coat of découpage medium.

Savory Barley-Mushroom Bake

Makes 8 servings

2 T. butter
1 onion, diced
1 c. mushrooms, chopped
1 c. pearled barley, uncooked
1/2 c. pine nuts or slivered
  almonds

2 green onions, thinly sliced
1/2 c. fresh parsley, chopped
1/4 t. salt
1/8 t. pepper
2 14-1/2 oz. cans vegetable or
  chicken broth

Melt butter in a skillet over medium-high heat. Stir in onion, mushrooms, uncooked barley and nuts. Cook and stir until barley is lightly golden, about 4 to 5 minutes. Stir in green onions and parsley; season with salt and pepper. Spoon mixture into a lightly greased 2-quart casserole dish; stir in broth. Cover and bake at 350 degrees for one hour and 15 minutes, or until barley is tender and broth has been absorbed.

Serve up a Southern-style vegetable plate for dinner.
With two or three scrumptious veggie dishes and
a basket of buttery cornbread, no one will even
miss the meat.

Vegetable Patch Pot Pie

Makes 6 servings

1 onion, chopped
8-oz. pkg. sliced mushrooms
1 clove garlic, minced
2 T. olive oil
3 c. vegetable broth
2 carrots, peeled and diced
2 potatoes, peeled and diced
2 stalks celery, sliced
2 c. cauliflower flowerets

1 c. green beans, trimmed and
   snapped into 1/2-inch pieces
1 t. kosher salt
1 t. pepper
2 T. cornstarch
2 T. soy sauce
1/4 c. water
2 9-inch pie crusts

In a skillet over medium heat, cook onion, mushrooms and garlic in oil for
3 to 5 minutes, stirring frequently. Stir in broth and remaining vegetables
Bring to a boil; reduce heat and simmer. Cook until vegetables are just tender,
about 5 minutes. Season with salt and pepper. In a small bowl, combine
cornstarch, soy sauce and water; mix until cornstarch has dissolved. Stir
cornstarch mixture into vegetables; simmer until sauce thickens. Roll out
one crust and place in an ungreased 11"x7" baking pan. Spoon filling
evenly over pastry. Roll out remaining crust and arrange over filling; crimp
edges. Bake at 425 degrees for 30 minutes, or until crust is golden.

A fresh-tasting chopped salad of lettuce and tomatoes is always welcome alongside spicy Mexican dishes. Try this easy dressing. In a covered jar, combine 3 tablespoons olive oil, 2 tablespoons lime juice, 1/4 teaspoon dry mustard and 1/2 teaspoon salt. Cover and shake until well blended.

Mexican Vegetable Casserole

Makes 6 to 8 servings

15-1/2 oz. black beans, drained
    and rinsed
14-1/4 oz. can corn, drained
10-oz. can diced tomatoes with
    green chiles
8-oz. container sour cream
8-oz. jar chunky salsa
2 c. cooked brown rice

8-oz. pkg. shredded Cheddar
    cheese
1/4 t. pepper
4-oz. can sliced black olives,
    drained
8-oz. pkg. shredded Pepper
    Jack cheese

Combine all ingredients except olives and Pepper Jack cheese; mix well.
Transfer to a lightly greased 13"x9" baking pan; top with olives and Pepper
Jack cheese. Bake, uncovered, at 350 degrees for 45 minutes, or until
bubbly and cheese is melted.

Did you know you can freeze casseroles baked or unbaked?
It's best to let the surface of the casserole freeze, then
wrap the entire baking pan tightly with plastic wrap or
aluminum foil. Don't forget to add some extra time to
the original baking directions.

Mom's Butternut Squash Bake

Serves 6 to 8

10-3/4 oz. can cream of
   chicken soup
1 c. sour cream
1 c. carrots, peeled and shredded
2 lbs. butternut squash, cooked
   and lightly mashed
1/4 c. onion, chopped
8-oz. pkg. herb-flavored
   stuffing mix
1/2 c. butter, melted

In a bowl, combine soup and sour cream. Stir in carrots; fold in squash and onion. Set aside. Combine stuffing mix and butter; spread 1/2 of mixture in bottom of a lightly greased 3-quart casserole dish. Spoon in squash mixture; top with remaining stuffing mix. Bake, uncovered, at 350 degrees for 25 to 30 minutes.

Did you know that if you add 1/2 teaspoon uncooked rice to a salt shaker, it keeps the salt from clogging in the shaker?

20-Minute Veggie Bake

Serves 4 to 6

8-oz. pkg. elbow macaroni, cooked
1 onion, chopped
1/2 c. celery, chopped
1 green pepper, chopped
8-oz. can sliced mushrooms, drained
1/4 c. oil
garlic salt to taste

1 t. salt
1/4 t. pepper
1/2 c. green olives with pimentos, chopped
6-oz. can tomato paste
1 c. water
1/2 c. grated Parmesan cheese

Spread cooked macaroni in a lightly greased 2-quart casserole dish; set aside. In a skillet, sauté onion, celery, green pepper and mushrooms in oil until tender. Add seasonings, olives, tomato paste and water; simmer for 10 minutes. Pour over macaroni; top with cheese. Bake, uncovered, at 375 degrees for 20 minutes, or until hot and bubbly.

A quick fall craft for kids...hot glue large acorn caps
onto round magnets for whimsical fridge magnets.

Carly's Green Bean Casserole

Makes 6 to 8 servings

1 lb. fresh green beans, trimmed
    and cut into bite-size pieces
10-3/4 oz. can cream of celery
    soup

1/2 c. plus 2 T. milk
1 c. slivered almonds, divided

Place beans in a buttered 1-1/2 quart casserole dish. Add soup, milk and 1/2 cup almonds; stir thoroughly. Top with remaining almonds. Bake, uncovered, at 375 degrees for 30 minutes, or until hot and bubbly.

Salt & pepper shakers make the best bud vases!
They're just the right size and come in so many
whimsical styles.

Savory Baked Potatoes

Serves 6

5 to 6 russet potatoes, very thinly sliced and divided
1/4 c. extra-virgin olive oil, divided
2 t. garlic powder
2 t. seasoned salt
1/2 t. celery salt
2 t. salt
2 t. pepper
Garnish: dried parsley

Arrange half of the potato slices in a greased 13"x9" glass baking pan. Drizzle with half of the oil. Combine all seasonings except garnish; sprinkle half of mixture over potatoes. Repeat layers; sprinkle parsley on top. Cover with aluminum foil. Bake at 375 degrees for 35 to 45 minutes, until potatoes are tender.

You can always use another tasty way to serve zucchini!
Choose medium zucchini...they're more tender than
the really large ones.

Scalloped Zucchini

4 to 5 zucchini, sliced and divided
1 onion, sliced and divided
10 to 12 slices pasteurized process
    cheese spread, divided

1 sleeve rectangular buttery
    crackers, crushed
1/2 c. butter, sliced

Layer half each of zucchini, onion and cheese slices in a buttered
13"x9" baking pan. Repeat layering; top with crackers and dot with
butter. Bake, uncovered, at 325 degrees until zucchini is tender, about
40 minutes, until bubbly and golden.

A cherished family recipe can be a super conversation starter. Take time to share family stories and traditions with your kids over the dinner table!

Granny's Sweet Potato Casserole

Serves 6

2-1/2 lbs. sweet potatoes, peeled
   and cubed
3/4 c. brown sugar, packed
1/4 c. butter, softened
1-1/2 t. salt

1/2 t. vanilla extract
1/2 c. pecans, finely chopped
   and divided
2 c. mini marshmallows

In a Dutch oven, cover sweet potatoes with cold water. Bring to a boil over high heat; reduce heat to medium. Simmer for 15 minutes, or until very tender; drain. Transfer potatoes to a large bowl and cool slightly. Add brown sugar, butter, salt and vanilla; mash mixture with a potato masher. Fold in 1/4 cup pecans. Spread evenly in an 11"x7" baking pan coated with non-stick vegetable spray. Sprinkle with remaining pecans; top with marshmallows. Bake, uncovered, at 375 degrees for 25 minutes, or until golden.

Fill a garden bell jar with clementines, pomegranates and shiny green apples. Cover the opening with a plate and turn right-side up. A centerpiece in no time at all!

Hot Fruit Casserole

Makes 8 to 10 servings

20-oz. jar applesauce
21-oz. can cherry pie filling
20-oz. can pineapple tidbits,
    drained
15-oz. can apricot halves, drained
    and cut into quarters
15-oz. can sliced pears, drained
    and cut into bite-size pieces

15-oz. can sliced peaches, drained
    and cut into bite-size pieces
1-1/2 c. light brown sugar, packed
1 T. cinnamon
Optional: 1/4 to 1/2 c. sherry

Spread applesauce in an ungreased 13"x9" glass baking pan; top with pie
filling. Layer remaining fruits over pie filling; set aside. Combine brown
sugar and cinnamon in a bowl; sprinkle over fruit mixture. Drizzle with
sherry, if using. Bake, uncovered, at 325 degrees for one hour, until hot
and bubbly. Serve warm.

Wrap and freeze small amounts of leftover cheeses. They may become crumbly when thawed, but will still be delicious in baked dishes.

Famous White Mac & Cheese

Makes 8 servings

16-oz. pkg. elbow macaroni,
    uncooked
2 T. butter
2 T. all-purpose flour

3 c. milk
1 lb. Monterey Jack cheese, cubed
1/2 lb. Pepper Jack cheese, cubed

Cook macaroni according to package directions; drain and set aside.
Meanwhile, melt butter in a saucepan over medium heat. Stir in flour
until combined; add milk and stir until mixture boils. Remove from heat;
add cheese and stir until melted. Combine cheese mixture and cooked
macaroni; spoon into an ungreased 13"x9" baking pan. Bake, uncovered,
at 350 degrees for 30 minutes, or until bubbly.

If you're baking a casserole at home before taking it to a potluck, keep it piping-hot by wrapping the baking pan in a layer of aluminum foil, then top with layers of newspaper.

Corny Popper Casserole

2 15-oz. cans corn, drained
1 red pepper, diced
2 T. jalapeño peppers, diced
1/2 c. butter, melted

1 c. whipping cream
1/2 c. milk
salt and pepper to taste

Combine all ingredients in a bowl. Mix well; transfer to a lightly greased 13"x9" baking pan. Bake, uncovered, at 375 degrees for 25 minutes. Stir before serving.

Save time when baking...tuck a measuring cup into your
countertop canisters. It'll be ready to scoop out
flour and sugar in a jiffy.

Peach Puff Cobbler

Serves 6 to 8

29-oz. can sliced peaches, drained
    and 1/2 c. syrup reserved
1/2 c. brown sugar, packed
2 t. lemon juice
1 c. biscuit baking mix

1/3 c. evaporated milk
2 T. sugar
2 t. butter, diced
Garnish: cinnamon-sugar

Combine reserved syrup, brown sugar and lemon juice in a saucepan.
Bring to a boil over medium-high heat; stir until brown sugar is dissolved.
Add peaches; remove from heat. In a bowl, stir together biscuit mix, milk
and sugar until dough forms. Spread dough in a greased 8"x8" baking pan.
Pour hot peach mixture over dough; dot with butter. Sprinkle with
cinnamon-sugar. Bake, uncovered, at 450 degrees for 15 to 20 minutes,
until bubbly and golden. Serve warm or cold.

Baking together is a fun family activity for kids just starting to learn how to cook. As you measure and mix together, be sure to share any stories about hand-me-down recipes. You'll be creating memories as well as sweet treats!

Healthy Oatmeal Apple Crisp   *Makes 8 servings*

6 c. tart apples, cored and sliced
1/4 c. frozen apple juice
   concentrate, thawed
1 t. cinnamon, divided
1/4 c. butter, softened

3/4 c. quick-cooking oats,
   uncooked
1/4 c. whole-wheat flour
1/3 c. brown sugar, packed

In a bowl, combine apples, apple juice concentrate and 1/2 teaspoon cinnamon. Stir until well mixed. Spread in an 8"x8" glass baking pan sprayed with non-stick vegetable spray. In the same bowl, mix remaining cinnamon and other ingredients until crumbly; sprinkle over apples. Bake, uncovered, at 375 degrees for 25 to 35 minutes, until apples are tender and topping is golden.

Fruit desserts are extra special topped with dollops of
whipped cream. In a chilled bowl, with chilled beaters,
whip a cup of whipping cream until soft peaks form.
Mix in 2 teaspoons sugar and 2 teaspoons vanilla
extract...and enjoy!

Social Apple Betty

Serves 6

6 to 7 apples, peeled, cored,
    and sliced
cinnamon to taste
Optional: sugar to taste

1/2 c. butter, softened
1 c. brown sugar, packed
3/4 c. all-purpose flour

Arrange sliced apples in an ungreased 1-1/2 quart casserole dish, filling 2/3 full. Sprinkle with cinnamon to taste. If apples are tart, add sugar as desired. In a bowl, blend butter and brown sugar. Add flour; mix with a fork until crumbly. Sprinkle butter mixture over apples; pat firmly into a crust. Bake at 325 degrees for 40 minutes, or until golden and apples are tender. Serve warm.

Invite family & friends to a dessert social. Everyone brings
a pie, a cake or another favorite dessert...you provide
the ice cream for topping and a pot of hot coffee.
Sure to be delicious fun!

Warm Banana Bread Cobbler

Serves 12

1-1/2 c. self-rising flour, divided
1 c. sugar
3/4 c. milk
1/2 c. butter, melted
1 t. vanilla extract
4 ripe bananas, sliced

1 c. rolled oats, uncooked
3/4 c. brown sugar, packed
1/2 c. butter, softened
1/2 c. chopped walnuts
Garnish: vanilla ice cream

In a bowl, stir together one cup flour and sugar. Add milk, melted butter and vanilla; stir until smooth. Spread batter evenly in a buttered rectangular 3-quart casserole dish. Top with sliced bananas; set aside. In a separate large bowl, combine oats, brown sugar and remaining flour. With a pastry cutter, cut in softened butter until crumbly; stir in walnuts. Sprinkle mixture over bananas. Bake at 375 degrees for 25 to 30 minutes, until set and golden. Serve warm, topped with ice cream.

Eggs work best in baking recipes when they're brought to
room temperature first. If time is short, just slip
the eggs carefully into a bowl of lukewarm water and
let stand for 15 minutes...they'll warm right up.

LaRae's Pumpkin Dump Cake

Serves 8 to 10

29-oz. can pumpkin
12-oz. can evaporated milk
4 eggs, beaten
1-1/2 c. sugar
1 t. cinnamon

1 t. ground ginger
1 t. ground cloves
1/2 t. salt
18-1/4 oz. pkg. yellow cake mix
1 c. butter, melted

Mix together pumpkin, milk, eggs, sugar, spices and salt with a whisk.
Spread in a greased 13"x9" baking pan. Sprinkle dry cake mix over top;
drizzle melted butter over all. Bake at 325 degrees for 1-1/2 hours.

Good things baked in the kitchen will keep romance
far longer than bright lipstick.

—Marjorie Husted

Triple Berry Crisp

Makes 8 servings

1 c. fresh blackberries
1 c. fresh blueberries
1 c. fresh raspberries
1 c. fresh pineapple, chopped
2 c. all-purpose flour

1 t. baking soda
1/2 t. cinnamon
1/4 t. ground ginger
1 T. honey
1/3 c. chilled butter

In an ungreased 2-quart casserole dish, combine berries and pineapple. Toss to mix and set aside. In a bowl, mix together flour, baking soda and spices. Cut in honey and butter until mixture is crumbly; sprinkle over berry mixture. Bake at 350 degrees for about 30 minutes, until crumbs start to turn golden.

INDEX

INDEX

Our Story

Back in 1984, we were next-door neighbors raising our families in the little town of Delaware, Ohio. Two moms with small children, we were looking for a way to do what we loved and stay home with the kids too. We had always shared a love of home cooking and making memories with family & friends and so, after many a conversation over the backyard fence, **Gooseberry Patch** was born.

We put together our first catalog at our kitchen tables, enlisting the help of our loved ones wherever we could. From that very first mailing, we found an immediate connection with many of our customers and it wasn't long before we began receiving letters, photos and recipes from these new friends. In 1992, we put together our very first cookbook, compiled from hundreds of these recipes and, the rest, as they say, is history.

Hard to believe it's been almost 40 years since those kitchen-table days! From that original little **Gooseberry Patch** family, we've grown to include an amazing group of creative folks who love cooking, decorating and creating as much as we do. Today, we're best known for our homestyle, family-friendly cookbooks, now recognized as national bestsellers.

One thing's for sure, we couldn't have done it without our friends all across the country. Each year, we're honored to turn thousands of your recipes into our collectible cookbooks. Our hope is that each book captures the stories and heart of all of you who have shared with us. Whether you've been with us since the beginning or are just discovering us, welcome to the **Gooseberry Patch** family!

Visit our website anytime
www.gooseberrypatch.com

JoAnn & Vickie

Email

1·800·854·6673